D1571563

EROS IN

Contemporary Gay
Poems About Sex

BOYSTOWN

Edited by
Michael Lassell

Crown Publishers, Inc.
New York

Published by Crown Publishers, Inc., 201 East 50th Street, New York, New York 10022. Member of the Crown Publishing Group.

Random House, Inc. New York, Toronto, London, Sydney, Auckland.

CROWN is a trademark of Crown Publishers, Inc.

Printed in the United States of America

Library of Congress Cataloging-in-Publication Data

Eros in Boystown : contemporary gay poems about sex / edited by
    Michael Lassell. — 1st ed.
      p.   cm.
    1. Erotic poetry, American.   2. Gay men's writings, American.
3. Gay men—Poetry.   I. Lassell, Michael, 1947– .
PS595.E76E76   1996
811′.50803538—dc20
95-34113
CIP

ISBN 0-517-70280-0

10 9 8 7 6 5 4 3 2 1

First Edition

This book is dedicated
to the memory of
Paul Monette
(1945–1995)

Friend, mentor,
poet, warrior

EROS IN
BOYSTOWN

GUILT, DESIRE AND LOVE

At the dark street corner
where Guilt and Desire
are attempting to stare
each other down
(presently, one of them
will light a cigarette
and glance in the direction
of the abandoned warehouse)
Love came slouching along,
an exploded silence
standing a little apart
but visible anyway
in the yellow, silent, steaming light,
while Guilt and Desire wrangled,
trying not to be overheard
by this trespasser.

Each time Desire looked towards Love,
hoping to find a witness,
Guilt shouted louder
and shook them hips
and the fire of the cigarette
threatened to burn the warehouse down.

Desire actually started across the street,
time after time,
to hear what Love might have to say,
but Guilt flagged down a truckload
of other people
and knelt down in the middle of the street
and, while the truckload of other people
looked away, and swore that they
didn't see nothing
and couldn't testify nohow,
and Love moved out of sight,
Guilt accomplished upon the standing body
of Desire
the momentary, inflammatory soothing
which seals their union
(for ever?)
and creates a mighty traffic problem.

THE BOY ON THE MAGAZINE COVER

In love with the boy/ on the magazine cover
His face all over town/ driving me crazy/
wanta wanta be with this boy's bronzed biceps,
Dishy delicious devilishly cute amazingly brilliant/
      breathtaking gorgeous beefcake,
playing with his G.I. Joe doll,
This hunk goes to extremes in love,
Wildly romantic aloof and indifferent he seems a bit
      scatty but there's no pulling the wool across his
      eyes.
He's a great fuck/ I just gotta get him into the sack;
That body language that face he's just plain gorgeous
      says he'll make an omelette for me in the morning.
They say he was bonking some guy/ when he wrote
      the song/
"Please don't break my heart"/ it goes,
I never never wanta say goodbye
to you/ your kisses/ you holdin' me tight/
to your untidy long blond locks
you utterly scrumptious absolutely gorgeous very
      hunky wonder boy
and versatile/ so versatile
well built slim ten and a half stone and single too/
      yummy.

MARK CLARK

walked with his hands
near his hips
like he wore guns
and was Wanted
in fifty states.
Out of the blue
something would tick him
and he'd attack
a friend, a girl,
whatever was near,
his face dark
as a rag pushed
onto a wound.
He was so alive then;
you had to desire
his wildness, his looks.

Even the coaches
let him pound
and bought him beers afterwards
and wanted to run him
for a week, train him,
be the one to bring him down.
And I, too,
in my room at night

dreamt of taming him
with my body, my mouth
so wet he would drink from it
like a kid does a hose
when he has been running all day
and must stop, must drink.

SECRET

my toes brush the blue
bottom of the pool
in Scott's backyard
as i tilt my head back
for an adolescent baptism.
my face accepts the sun as Scott
swims on his back
through my parted legs
while breathing out bubbles
that shimmer up my body
like butterflies,
like blinking eyes—
and when he bends beneath me
i straddle his shoulders
and rise like Poseidon
from a chlorine Aegean.
my calves note the hard
candy of his nipples as he
launches me skyward
and i strike the water—
a breaching dolphin.
later we bask on bleached beach towels
and Scott smears fruit-smelling sweetness
on my slim anxious back,
as specks of dirt scratch lines in the oil

between my skin and his fingers,
adding hopeful commas
to our tactile vocabulary.
my stomach tightens
and my vision blurs
from the sun and sweat and i
spill my lemonade
in the just-cut grass,
afraid he can feel my heart
about to beat through my ribcage
and leap into his supple hand
like one of the secrets
i think we're keeping.

TO AN ANGEL

The first time we meet
in New York City
it will be snowing.
No one will stop
to take a picture
of us as we stand
inches apart and shake
hands on a busy street
corner. Taxicabs
will continue to pass
splattering dirty slush
onto our wool coats.
We will walk
in silence to a cafe
where we'll sit
for hours sipping
espresso, fingering sugar
packets. The smoke
from your cigarette
will rise and hover
around your head
like mist in a grave-
yard covering
a tombstone at dawn,
the epitaph barely readable.

Just after midnight
you will lean forward,
your face—pale
and thin—emerging
from the haze, eyes
dark as skulls',
and slowly, unnoticed,
we will kiss.

TIM'S STOLEN SWEATER

Sunlight which seeps through a part
in the drapes illuminates the rumpled
contents of your suitcase: sweaters
and slacks, and some of those short-
sleeved alligator shirts, the kind
that "clones" wear, though they'd make
you look good—healthy and athletic—
unlike most of the men at the crowded
bar where we met. Before we spoke,
I wanted to reach across and touch
your cheekbone, the scar just under
the left one (I couldn't bring myself
to ask how you'd gotten it, so I
imagined a gang fight in your youth
or a steak knife in the hand of
a lover insane with jealousy). You
introduced yourself. I extended my
hand. Then, in your room, our chit-
chat continued until, abruptly, you
asked, "Do you want to kiss me?" It
was a perfect way to get to the point
and I was impressed. "Yes." Our move-
ments cast shadows of flesh barely
lit by the glow of the motel's neon
sign as it flashed on and off. Just

a few hours sleep. Now, slightly hung
over, I erase one or two of the creases
our bodies made in sheets a maid will
change later in the day, after we've
showered and dressed, gone our sep-
arate ways. You're going out for a
newspaper and a six-pack. I watch you
rummage through your suitcase, pull
on a pair of boxer shorts, jeans, and
the sweater you wore last night—
light blue with thin white stripes
around the chest—which is what I
noticed first, from across the bar,
and then, as I moved closer, how
handsome you were, despite your scar.

COLD FRONT

for Guillermo

Argentine breeze
    bending tropical trees
       legs taut   hardened cock
         Hurricane of kisses
       against darkening
     flesh   swirling hair
neck arched   Thickening clouds
 slip between sheets of rain
pages of thunder
     Strokes of
   lightning
  tightened ass
    clenched fist
      I clutch
       your body
        like a
       blind man
         for you are
        warm air
         spiraling
        thru
        me

NEW SONG OF SOLOMON

Look how we're wedded—
jubilant, unchecked.
The armoire mirror
is our witness:
this is a new Song of Solomon
we're fashioning;
in Tuscan niches
where our bed is green
or trophy-bright,
in shuttered
Florentine and Roman rooms,
your body has become
my refuge and intoxicant.

You've given me
rosemary, trumpet lilies, musk, God
in the hours of languor.
You've given me
calamus and cinnamon,
your hands' acumen.

I want the crush of your pelvis,
your outlaw kiss.
I want your inmost wonder,
your fierce mouth
here. And here.

THE ONLY LIVING MAN
IN THE WORLD

for David

In a world where every act must
be named and where every act has
no consequences, I can take
my man in my arms and smooch him
under the stars in the fog on top
of a hill overlooking the nightlights
of the city in which I love him
and call it a flowered cactus.

   He can tie me up and spit on me
in the act of love-making and I
will call it a yellow pearl. We
can devour all-you-can-eat rib dinners
all weekend and call it the drone of velvet.
We can delight in our isolation;
we can dodge the pinge of guilt or shame
or fear or boredom; we can be lovers
who return to a world to find friends
long gone, our homes burned to the ground,
our pets eaten, our families emigrated
to unpronounceable lands; we can burn
into the each other's psyche like a brand
on the butt of a prized steer, we can get
high pissed drunk stay up all night

and get stinky in each other's arms
and I will call it
the reckless hiss of our life together.

    I tell you that if you should leave me,
my heart will turn to deep sleep and somewhere
I shall dream of acts that I cannot name
but in the darkness of my heart and I shall
invent a language that sneaks your familiar,
your cherished body into the thorny terrain
of my blood. I will talk to barbed wire
and it will talk back to me.

HALFWAY

I hold you in my hand,
        my mouth,
        my mind:
you have my nipple,
        my earring,
        my phone number.
Take a breath: you're ready
        with your sad eyes,
        your crooked teeth.
From the highest floor, inside
        all the way,
        the waltz movement:
down to the lowest,
        the unmade bed,
        the used condom.
On the stairs, halfway:
        the long memory,
        the definite article.

HE INTERPRETS THE DREAM

The globe that you're exploring represents
My body. I'm the island—look at me,
How much I'm like your island, my bent knees
Pathetic mountains, my cock a monument
To some pathetic dictator, my thighs
Abandoned plazas where your father's said
You'll never play. The ocean is the bed
Hart Crane is sleeping in, an ocean high
And unitary which could drown the earth.
Instead, the earth begins to swell. It's clear
You want the earth to fuck you everywhere,
The way I do, to raise you from yourself,
Transport you there—I'm here, you mustn't be
Afraid. I'm resting like an island, home
Upon this sea of sheets—your metronome
A compass in my voice, the voice you seek.

LOVE POEM

On the narrow bed. Patterns of light
and shadow across your body. I hold

your face in my hands. Tell me, before
I kiss you, what is it like to be

so beautiful? I want to know how other
hands have touched you. What other

eyes, beneath your clothes, imagine.
And how do you imagine me? Do you

feel my calloused skin? See my twisted
bones? When you take off my clothes

will you kiss me all over? Touch me as
if my body were yours. Make me beautiful.

SAUDADE

Carioca boy,
new epithets would have
to be coined
to describe
the supple promises
your body makes
turning the air
electric
on Copacabana beach.
Waking up these mornings
even my toes
sing your name;
my dales and gullies
lodge the warmth
of your skin.
Carioca boy,
when I step onto the balcony
the dowdiest flowers
startle me;
the Jamaica beige
petals
of the begonias
are bounteous hands
reminding me
of the silkiness

of your caresses.
Carioca boy,
you're an unknown elixir,
you feed me forbidden fruits;
when we embrace
you drag me
to fathomless depths;
when we touch
I enter paradise.
All this happens,
Carioca boy,
when your carnal *saudade*
sets my lips
afire.

BYRON ALFONSO

The dance you did in the mirror nude   erect
the ancient Mayas might have done
    or the decadent Atlanteans
before the continent slipped
                                into the sea
the pagan dance
                    that bypassed time
    (ancient disco fever)

A god entered you
                as you entered me

old satyr and young faun
    sharing the mysteries
        bypassing laws
drunken-stoned temple dancer
young male whore
    reviving the ritual
        with cannabis

rubbing your smooth body
against my furry one

smell of goats and satyrs

                gleaming sweat

with each step
                and bent thigh
the god rises
                and resurrects

the grunting dance
                of erections

ST. MARKS PLACE

Outside the Puerto Ricans make calls all night
    on the street phones
and FOOD sells hot chicken and grease-fried light.
    Trucks down Second Avenue clatter in the rain

Here in our room the street
    is just a sound before dreaming

Past the pots and pot plants at the windows
    light shines in
so I can have your sleepy smile
    that excites me into calm

You move on me
    like someone from long ago
lost, and met again after lifetimes,
    smiling, comfortable, knowing you'd find me again
when I, worrier, feared you'd gone forever

I tell you: I love your freckled back,
    the holes in your clothes, your
sleep

Hold me in your smiley sigh
    awhile,

hold me while I take
    your cock in my head till my mouth aches
and your body feels the quietest thing of all,
    stiller than the clock, the water glass,

the shadows from the hall.
    We're home. Drifting in the ticking dark.
The tap trickles in the other room,
    quiet voices murmur through the walls

PUNK ROCK YOUR MY
BIG CRYBABY

I'll tell my deaf mother on you! Fall on the floor
and eat your grandmother's diapers! Drums,
Whatta lotta Noise you want a Revolution?
Wanna Apocalypse? Blow up in Dynamite Sound?
I can't get excited, Louder! Viciouser!
Fuck me in the ass! Suck me! Come in my ears!
I want those pink Abdominal bellybuttons!
Promise you'll murder me in the gutter with Orgasms!
I'll buy a ticket to your nightclub, I wanna get busted!
50 years old I wanna Go! with whips & chains &
        leather!
Spank me! Kiss me in the eye! Suck me all over
from Mabuhay Gardens to CBGB's coast to coast
Skull to toe Gimme yr electric guitar naked,
Punk President, eat up the FBI w/ yr big mouth.

D. BELLAMY

Ed sucking me at the baths, everyone looking, scraped my nipple, hey watch out, then pounded my heart once with his fist. I kiddingly leaned back as if stunned but actually found myself fainting till I blacked out & into a rising and welling & dared myself to follow it though I might be dying & felt reckless & struggled higher into the tumult & roaring thinking at the same time the headline in tomorrow's paper would be about me and sordid. I look down—I'm floating—Ed still sucks the cock of my fainted self, I'm held by this, my cock about 15 feet long & knotted in places & I bob at the end. "Now I am totally alienated from my body. This might be a good time to stop and think." In the distance of my distant tip a frail star of sensual feeling.

PORNOGRAPHIC POEM (1965)

Seven Cuban
army officers
in exile
were at me
all night.
Tall,
sleek,
slender
Spanish types
with smooth dark
muscular bodies
and hair
like wet coal
on their heads
and between their legs.
I lost count
of the times
I was fucked
by them
in every conceivable
position.

At one point
they stood
around me
in a circle
and I had
to crawl
from one crotch
to another
sucking
on each cock
until it was hard.
When I got all
seven up
I shivered
looking up
at those erect pricks
all different lengths
and widths
and knowing
that each one
was going up

my ass hole.
Everyone
of them
came
at least twice
and some three times.
Once they put me
on the bed
kneeling,
one fucked me
in the behind,
another
in the mouth,
while I jacked off
one
with each hand
and two
of the others
rubbed
their peckers
on my bare feet
waiting
their turns
to get
into my can.
Just when I thought
they were all spent
two of them
got together
and fucked me
at once.
The positions
we were in
were crazy
but with two
big fat
Cuban cocks
up my ass
at one time
I was
in paradise.

(UNTITLED)

What—I wanted to ask—is your wildest fantasy?
This to a semi-clothed man on the heath at Hampstead
A man surrounded by other men
Some with their cocks loose in the air
Some stroking his skin
Touching hair
Feeling nipples
Stroking body
Wanking cock
I saw a shine in his eyes
And stretched out my hand
Exploring the hair on his chest
Down his belly into groin
His arms enfold me
Hands feeling the shape of chest and waist
Fingers loosen my flies
Unfasten my trousers
Release my hard cock
I am only conscious of his strong fingers
Gently probing
Discovering
Moist, expectant areas
A mouth—not his—begins to suck
His right hand rhythmically strokes my body
His left hand ripples up my back

Reaches round to my right nipple
As my back arches in climax
My right hand grasps his chest
He holds me still
In the damp, misty, early spring air.

THEME AND VIOLATIONS

Noticing you beautifully breaking the law
by sitting cross-ankled on the Esplanade
wall, I exposed myself indecently
in public response to nature's purest call.
Lawlessly, I loitered on the bridge
you crossed over, headed for the bushes,
where I lewdly and lasciviously laid
both hands on your most private parts.
We arrested our attentions immediately,
each sentencing the other heavily to
from one night to unnumbered years of lively
lovemaking in his own enclosing arms,
with the penalty added of an early parole
in the case, only, of too much control.

THE SECRET OF BLUE

The secret of blue is well kept. Blue comes from far away. On its way, it hardens and changes into a mountain. The cicada works at it. The birds assist. In reality, one doesn't know. One speaks of Prussian blue. In Naples, the virgin stays in the cracks of walls when the sky recedes.

But it's all a mystery. The mystery of sapphire, mystery of Sainte Vierge, mystery of the siphon, mystery of the sailor's collar, mystery of the blue rays that blind and your blue eye which goes through my heart.

TRANSLATED BY JEREMY REED

THINGS ARE STILL SUDDEN
& WONDERFUL

Once it was 1962 & somebody
kissed you you freaked he

held you down pressed his
15-yr.-old football team thighs   hard

against yr. thin-kid-with-glasses
legs   It was like a Lana Turner movie

; you decided to be gay. In 1982 yr. lover
puts you down on all fours & masturbates

you sometimes you come with a leash on
in more than one room. You've

not forgotten the football player's name

THE PIERCING

A biker did the trick
white snow-
addicted angelic
placed one rough hand
(fresh from the grip of his Harley)
onto my brown biceps
squeezed me man-hard
as he guided the steel needle
through my nipple
rigid in the bite of forceps.
"You okay, baby?"
That was no question.

My lover looked on
oh so
aware of this surgical subtext
fucking with instruments
thrilled at the vision
of my tongue
thick and spit-heavy
shining the boots of Jimmy Dean.
Was this the ménage of which we'd spoken?

The pain was like lightning
when he entered me.

The violence of his caress
split me like a tree
severed in the fury of an April storm.
(I remained hard for days.)

Now this ring this circle jerk.

This must be faggot alchemy.
He instructs as wizard to apprentice:
       Flesh turns silver to gold.
       Blood keeps silver sterling and true.
       The yin. The yang.

In his grip
I am a teenager again
innocent and pure
strapped to a rack at the Mineshaft
one naked bulb-lit night.
A simple time
before all my dreams came true
and I woke up
rich blond meteoric.

In an antique porcelain tub I lay
ready for harness for bridle for riding

crop
ferocious id snarls unleashed
pitbulls sense this bitch's heat
nazis, bikers.

He instructs as wizard to apprentice:
       Each night with purest of cotton—ablution.
       Each night when the moon rings high—
          rotation.
       The yin. The yang.

In this way I
was healed
became holy
grew a third eye
come to testify. . . .

COMING TRUE

Having wanted him for
so long, inventing weak
excuses to phone and
            contriving

to bump into him at
the shops or out drinking,
having what I wanted
            I can't cope.

What I used to wet the
sheets dreaming of doing
I now do often at
            his request

and what I ask for in
return I no longer
have to beg the pillow
            for in vain.

How can I even think
of sleeping when I've just
exhausted any dreams
            I might have

had, yelping in the damp
behind his balls? Darkness
could never remedy
            this turmoil.

TURMOIL

Night after pungent night
we sweat, march through the city
hard and fast, unable to catch our breath.
Our bodies strike against each other,
shoulder to shoulder.
We could throw sparks up the dry hills,
Silverlake, LAX, the 101 ignited.
Thousands spurred by Sparklet's drums and bullhorns.
Our chrome whistles gleam under the moon,
children watch from bedroom windows,
some flip us off.
My lover and I are driven to sex now
four, five times a week.
I rub his moist, sore back,
the sweat lubrication,
tension removed from skin and sinew.
I admit I want to get belted,
parts of my body chewed,
to be told how I taste.

His chest I've shaved bare,
sharp razor, mentholated foam.
I treat his skin like a young boy's.
He lets me drift into sleep,
his pulse curls up along my back.

I imagine fire past the curtains,
a steady stream of molten earth,
rocks thrown through windows.
I kick away the sheets,
his arm is pressed around my waist
as if to never let go.
I want God to see this, unhindered,
what he created,
the mingle of flame and brawn
to smell the muscles of this love.

BIG LOAD PRIDE

Boy proud of the big load
        he just shot off
        in his friend's mouth,
Delighted he came so much—
        more than ever!
Delighted by the gulping
        almost choking hungry mouth,
The cocksucker transfigured by
So much boycome
        ejaculated into his being!
The boy giddy, being made
        so much lighter,
        his balls float free—
Don't you think he wants
As much semen to shoot
        from his cock
        as possible,
The bigger the load the better,
Coming so much in one blowjob
His ripe balls drained
From super-full to empty
        from a single
        heavy-duty suck?

(UNTITLED)

Your eyes fell upon my skin
embarrassed
delighted
you were clothed
I was naked
intimacy new to us
I was young
cradled soft in your palms
I was your master
you were drawn to me
I held your eyes
you held mine
smiles
trembling lips
we were young
intimacy new to us
embarrassed
excited
the night was young
we cradled soft in its hours
it was our master
we were drawn into the night

DANCER(S) WITH DICK(S) AT THE 1 SALOON KEY WEST, FLORIDA

I have one hand on his cock, the other
deeply involved with the shaven every-
thing between his balls and asshole, at which

willing target I've aimed my spit-slick thumb.
"All *right*," he says, bending to help me and
offer a kiss, "work *me!*" I don't want to

disappoint, so I pop one proffered tit
in my mouth while he grinds that totally
tubular rod of his into my palm.

"My name is Chris," he says (he's a solo
tonight—the other dancer's father had
a stroke). "You *are* a hot daddy," he says,

which takes me aback (I feel twenty-six
most of the time). I give him another
buck: "I guess I'm getting there," I shuffle.

"No getting there involved," he says, his brown
forehead a furrow, "you have *arrived*." I
take him at his word—after all, he's the

pro. He might just be right. So, now I'm a
daddy, I think, and let it sink slowly
in. Well, it's better than nothing, I guess—

here at the far end of further away
than anywhere and way beyond what the
hell. You know what I mean, pretty baby?

AMERICAN BOY

I do not seek you out
        For if I do
You say I might get tired of you.
        To think I was afraid
You'd be the one to tire while we both still
        Warm to the naked thrill
Precisely of that strangeness that has made
        For such self-doubt.

I hated those old men
        With turkey-necks
And undiminished love of sex,
        The curtains of their skin
Tripping them up at their incautious play,
        When out of torpor they
Had woken as ambitious as if in
        Their prime again.

Now I myself am old
        We calculate
Our games for such and such a date.
        Like bicoastal romance,
In which one night a quarter is the most
        Spared to the other coast,

Ours thrives as we stretch out our ignorance:
　　Men of the world.

　　Affectionate young man,
　　　Your wisdom feeds
　My dried-up impulses, my needs,
　　With energy and juice.
Expertly you know how to maintain me
　　At the exact degree
Of hunger without starving. We produce
　　What warmth we can.

James   Broughton

TWO ADAMS IN A
SONOMA WOOD

Under the windsong of the redwood trees
we were two Adams together clinging
in the long nakedness of afternoon

Rediscovering close harmony
fingers practiced fresh arpeggios
nipples shone from riper torsos
loins opened into full bloom
Never had sweat tasted so juicy
or prolonged kiss so penetrant

Who in Eden lives for fashion
for investment   for notoriety?
Who is planning to go anywhere?

Reciprocal in savoring
we explored carnal phenomena
murmured unsayable secrets
tossed raptures back and forth
drank from each other's auras
till we purred with the hum of the world

Two seasoned lovers clinging together
renewed their Adamness on a bed of fern
under the windsong of the ancient trees

THE ROMAN BATHS AT NÎMES

In the hall of mirrors nobody speaks.
An ember smolders before hollowed cheeks.
Someone empties pockets, loose change and keys,
into a locker. My god, forgive me.
Some say love, disclosed, repels what it sees,
yet if I touch the darkness, it touches me.
In the steamroom, inconsolable tears
fall against us. In the whirlpool, my arms
rowing through little green crests, help to steer
the body, riding against death. Yet what harm
is there in us? I swear to you, my friend,
crossarmed in a bright beach towel, turning round
to see my face in lamplight, that eye, ear
and tongue, good things, make something sweet of
        fear.

THE GIFT

It was Auden that gave me away, you said,
Alone in the carriage at the end of the line,
Pretending to read. Later, our bed
The golf course, under the moon

And the jittery leaves, you asked my name,
First, before we kissed, undressed.
I could barely see your face, though your frame
Was clear against the grass, and I guessed

I might never meet you again. But stretched
On the well-kept lawn that summer night,
Two strangers shared each other, touched:
A gift essential as love, or sight.

LULLABY

Lay your sleeping head, my love,
Human on my faithless arm;
Time and fevers burn away
Individual beauty from
Thoughtful children, and the grave
Proves the child ephemeral:
But in my arms till break of day
Let the living creature lie,
Mortal, guilty, but to me
The entirely beautiful.

Soul and body have no bounds:
To lovers as they lie upon
Her tolerant enchanted slope
In their ordinary swoon,
Grave the vision Venus sends
Of supernatural sympathy,
Universal love and hope;
While an abstract insight wakes
Among the glaciers and the rocks
The hermit's carnal ecstasy.

Certainty, fidelity
On the stroke of midnight pass
Like vibrations of a bell

And fashionable madmen raise
Their pedantic boring cry:
Every farthing of the cost,
All the dreaded cards foretell,
Shall be paid, but from this night
Not a whisper, not a thought,
Not a kiss nor look be lost.

Beauty, midnight, vision dies:
Let the winds of dawn that blow
Softly round your dreaming head
Such a day of welcome show
Eye and knocking heart may bless,
Find our mortal world enough;
Noons of dryness find you fed
By the involuntary powers,
Nights of insult let you pass
Watched by every human love.

STEVE ANTHONY (b. 1958) edited *Of Eros and of Dust* (Oscars Press, 1992) and coedited (with Peter Daniels) *Jugular Defences* (Oscars Press, 1994). He lives in England.

ANTLER (b. 1946) is the winner of a Walt Whitman Award and a Pushcart Prize. He is the author of *Factory* (City Lights, 1980) and *Last Words* (Ballantine, 1986).

W. H. AUDEN (1907–73) has been called the first authentically modern poet writing in English. He was the most influential of a circle that included Christopher Isherwood and Stephen Spender.

JAMES BALDWIN (1924–87) was an internationally acclaimed novelist, playwright, essayist, and poet. His works include *Go Tell It on the Mountain* (1953), *Giovanni's Room* (1956), and *Blues for Mr. Charlie* (1964).

MARK BIBBINS (b. 1968) lives in New York City. His work has appeared in *The Paris Review, The Badboy Book of Erotic Poetry* (Masquerade, 1995), and elsewhere.

WALTA BORAWSKI (1947–94) was the author of *Sexually Dangerous Poet* (Good Gay Poets, 1984) and *Lingering in a Silk Shirt* (Fag Rag Books, 1994). He died of complications from AIDS in 1994.

JAMES BROUGHTON (b. 1913) has received two Guggenheim and two NEA grants. His recent publications include *Special Deliveries* (Broken Moon Press, 1990).

REGIE CABICO (b. 1970) is the winner of the 1993 New York Poetry Slam. His work appears in *Aloud: Voices from The Nuyorican Poets Cafe* (Henry Holt, 1994) and *The Name of Love* (St. Martin's Press, 1995).

RAFAEL CAMPO (b. 1964) is the author of *The Other Man Was Me* (Arte Público Press, 1994), which won the 1993 National Poetry Series Award. He is a graduate of Harvard Medical School.

CYRUS CASSELLS (b. 1957) is the author of *The Mud Actor* (Henry Holt, 1982), a National Poetry Series selection, and *Soul Make a Path Through Shouting* (Copper Canyon, 1994).

JUSTIN CHIN (b. 1969) is a writer and performance artist. He lives in San Francisco.

JEAN COCTEAU (1889–1963) was an artist, photographer, theater designer, and filmmaker (*The Blood of a Poet*, 1930; *Beauty and the Beast*, 1946), as well as a poet and novelist.

HENRI COLE (b. 1956) is the author of *The Marble Queen* (Athenaeum, 1986), *The Zoo Wheel of Knowledge* (Alfred A. Knopf, 1989), and *The Look of Things* (Alfred A. Knopf, 1995).

JEFFERY CONWAY (b. 1964) lives in New York City. His work has appeared in *Columbia Poetry Review, The Portable Lower East Side,* and *B City.* His chapbook, *Blood Poisoning,* is from Cold Calm Press.

DENNIS COOPER (b. 1953) is the author of the novels *Closer* (1989), *Frisk* (1991), and *Try* (1994), all published by Grove Press. His latest collection of poetry, *The Dream Police,* was published by Grove/Atlantic in 1995.

GIL CUADROS (b. 1962) is the author of *City of God* (City Lights, 1994). His work has appeared in *High Risk 2* (Plume, 1994) and *Indivisible* (Plume, 1991).

PETER DANIELS (b. 1954) is the author of *Peacock Luggage* (1992) and *Be Prepared,* both from Smith/Doorstop of Huddersfield, England. For the Oscars Press he coedited with Steve Anthony *Jugular Defences: An AIDS Anthology* (1994).

GAVIN GEOFFREY DILLARD (b. 1954), long known as "the naked poet," is a writer, artist, and erotic film star.

KENNY FRIES (b. 1960) is the author of *The Healing Notebooks* (Open Books, 1990) and *Body, Remember,* a memoir. He is editor of a forthcoming anthology of work by writers who live with physical disabilities.

ALLEN GINSBERG (b. 1926) has been a central fixture of arts and letters since the publication of *Howl and Other Poems* (City Lights Books, 1956).

JOHN GIORNO (b. 1935) originated spoken word and performance poetry and was the star of Andy Warhol's *Sleep.* His most recent book is *You Got to Burn to Shine: New and Selected Writings* (Serpent's Tail, 1994).

ROBERT GLÜCK (b. 1947) is the author of *Margery Kempe* (High Risk/Serpent's Tail, 1994), *Jack the Modernist* (republished by High Risk/Serpent's Tail, 1995), and *Reader* (Lapis Press, 1989).

THOM GUNN (b. 1929) lives in San Francisco. His recent books are *The Man With Night Sweats* (1992) and *Collected Poems* (1994), both by Farrar, Straus, and Giroux.

MARTIN HUMPHRIES (b. 1955) is the author of three collections of poetry and was the editor of the Gay Men's Press verse series. He lives in London.

CARY ALAN JOHNSON (b. 1960) is a Brooklyn-born writer who has lived and worked extensively in Africa. His work has appeared in *The Road Before Us* (1991) and *Here to Dare* (1992), both published by Galiens Press.

CHRIS JONES (b. 1956) is an Australian activist and a video-maker (working with *Queer TV,* Sydney). He is the author of *The Times of Zenia Gold* (Blackwattle Press, 1992).

RUDY KIKEL (b. 1942) is the author of *Lasting Relations* (Sea Horse Press, 1984) and *Long Division* (Writers Block, 1992).

MICHAEL LASSELL (b. 1947) is the author of *Poems for Lost and Un-lost Boys* (Amelia, 1985), *Decade Dance* (Alyson, 1990), and *The Hard Way* (A

Richard Kasak Book, 1995), as well as the editor of *The Name of Love: Classic Gay Love Poems* (St. Martin's Press, 1995).

JAIME MANRIQUE (b. 1949) was born in Colombia, where his first volume of poetry received the National Poetry Award in 1975. He is the author of *Latin Moon in Manhattan* (St. Martin's Press, 1992).

HAROLD NORSE (b. 1916) is the author of twelve books of poetry, including *The Carnivorous Saint* (Gay Sunshine, 1977) and *Love Poems* (Crossing Press, 1986).

JEREMY REED (b. 1951; translator Cocteau) is a widely acclaimed British poet. He is the author of *Selected Poems* (Penguin, 1987), *Nineties* (Cape, 1990), and *Dicing for Pearls* (Enitharmon, 1990), as well as four novels.

DAVID TRINIDAD (b. 1953) is a native of Los Angeles who now lives in New York City. The most recent of his numerous books is *Answer Song* (High Risk/Serpent's Tail, 1994).

GREGORY WOODS (b. 1953) is the author of *Articulate Flesh: Male Homoeroticism and Modern Poetry* (Yale University Press, 1987) and an acclaimed collection of poems, *We Have the Melon* (Carcanet, 1992).

IAN YOUNG (b. 1945) is the author of *Sex Magick* (Stubblejumper Press, 1986) and *The Stonewall Experiment: A Gay Psychohistory* (Cassell, 1995). He is the editor of the groundbreaking anthologies *The Male Muse* (1973) and *Son of the Male Muse* (1983).